DINOSAURS

Modern Publishing
A Division of Unisystems, Inc.
New York, New York 10022

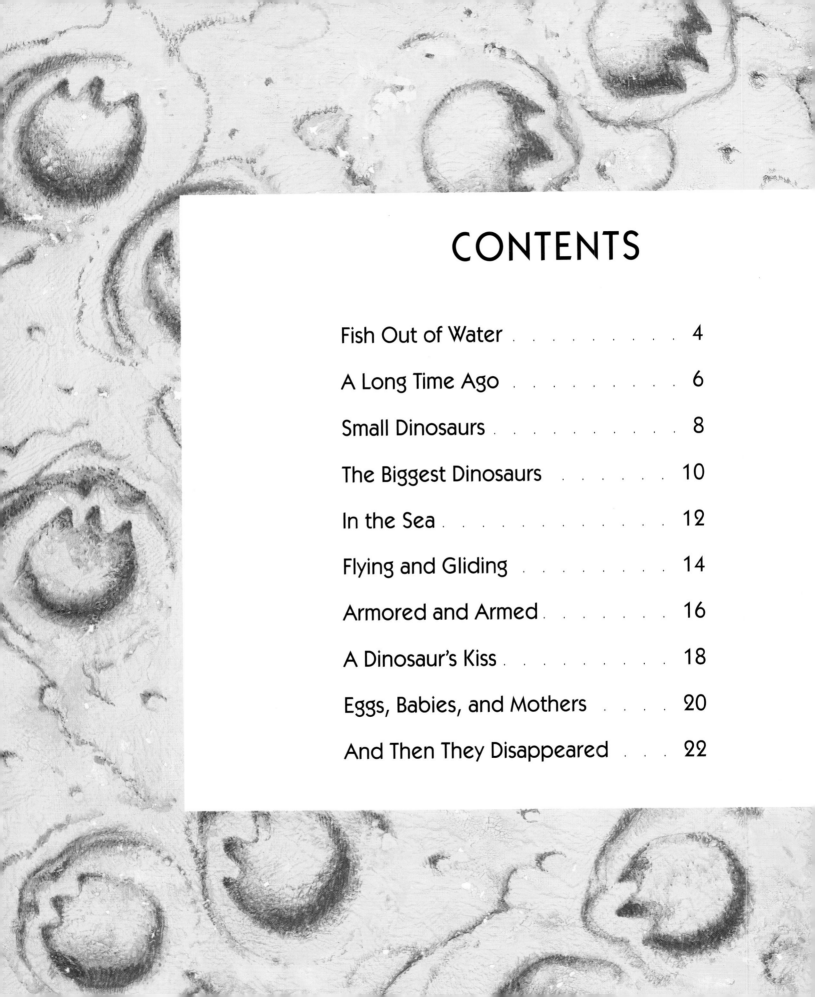

CONTENTS

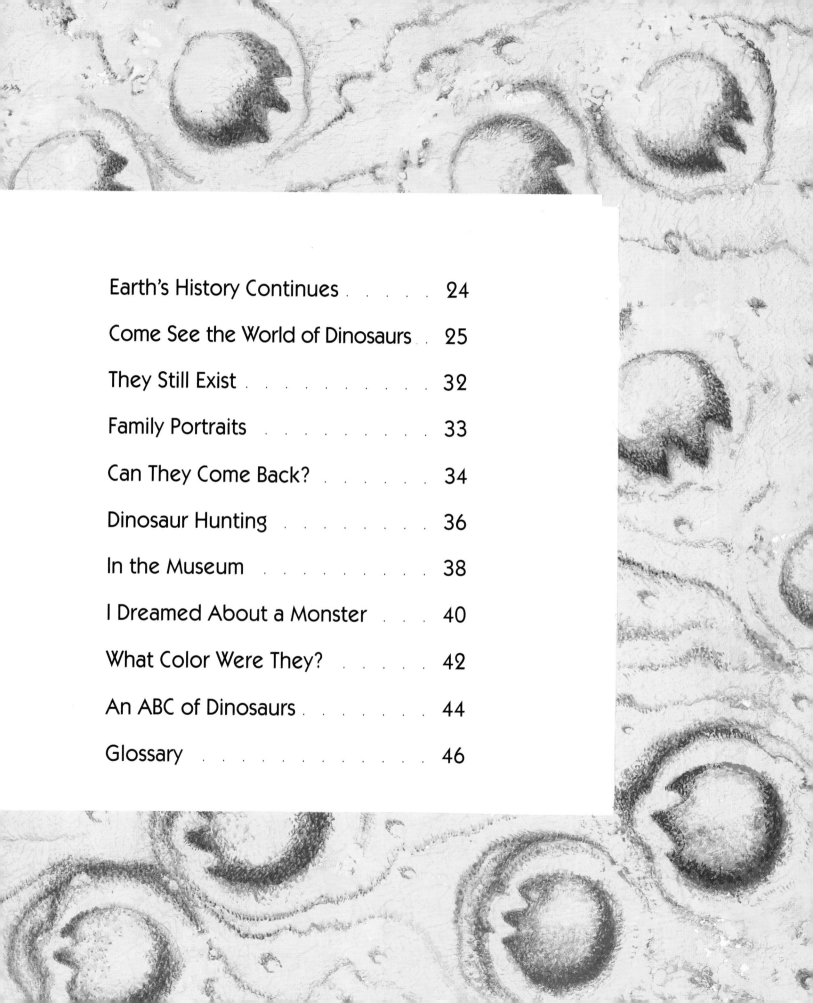

Fish Out of Water

Who Were the First?—Many millions of years ago some fish adapted, little by little to live on land, and they began to breathe air. Scientists guess that they might have looked something like the animal illustrated here.

A Long Time Ago

The First Plants on Earth— The first living things on the earth were like seaweed. They grew in the sea, which at that time was warm and covered most of the earth. Millions of years ago, some of the plants became slightly stiffer and able to survive on land. They continued to adapt by

growing long roots which anchored them firmly to the soil. By the time the first land animals appeared, the earth was already covered with plants.

A Double Life—From the first fish that were able to slither on land a new kind of animal evolved. These were "amphibians," which means "to have a double life." They began life as fish, breathing through gills. As adults they lived on land, breathing air through lungs. Amphibians are alive today: frogs. The young frogs or tadpoles look like fish, live in the water, and breathe through gills. The adult frogs swim in water but have lungs and so cannot breathe under water.

Reptiles—Another kind of animal evolved from the amphibians. These are the "reptiles," which means "to

The eryops was an ancestor of the crocodile.

creep." Reptiles laid eggs with hard shells. The eggs held the babies, along with a nutritious liquid that fed the babies and protected them from harm. The babies were born on land, and eventually reptiles evolved into land animals. The name reptile was first given to modern snakes and lizards. Now the name is also used to refer to some of the dinosaurs or "terrible lizards."

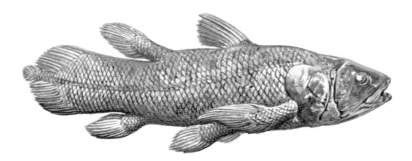

The Coelacanth is a fish that still exists today. It is very similar to its ancestors, which lived 300 million years ago. From fish of this kind (with fins like feet), the first amphibians evolved.

The tyrannosaurus rex was the largest of the carnivorous dinosaurs, also called "carnosaurs." It had very large, strong hind legs and a muscular tail. The front limbs, which divided into two "fingers," were so short that they could not reach the animal's large, toothy mouth. Although the tyrannosaurus rex looks very ferocious, scientists now believe the tyrannosaurus rex was a scavenger. It fed mostly on animals that had already been killed, just as hyenas and jackals do today.

Small Dinosaurs

Giants and Dwarfs—When we think of dinosaurs, we usually think of very large animals. Some dinosaurs were huge, but many were very small— the size of a chicken. These "dwarf" dinosaurs have been found in many different environments.

The bactrosaurus was a herbivore about as tall as a ten-year-old child.

The coelurus was a small and very agile herbivore.

Like a Pack of Wolves—Some of the small dinosaurs were carnivores. They were able to hunt large prey because they hunted in groups, like wolves do today. Scientists think these dinosaurs must have been very intelligent to be able to hunt so efficiently in groups.

What They Looked Like—The small two-legged dinosaurs had heads and tails like lizards, and claws like vultures. They could run very fast and used their claws as weapons. The herbivores had short flat teeth; the carnivores' teeth were long and daggerlike, good for holding on to the prey they caught.

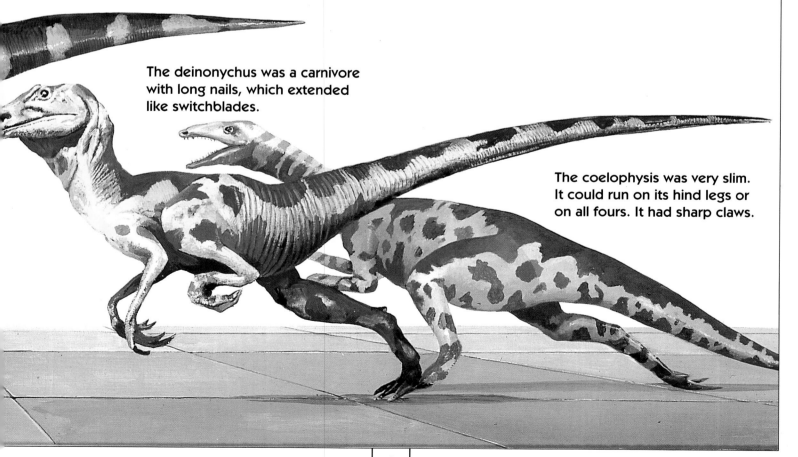

The deinonychus was a carnivore with long nails, which extended like switchblades.

The coelophysis was very slim. It could run on its hind legs or on all fours. It had sharp claws.

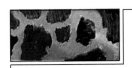

The Biggest Dinosaurs

Animal Giants—The biggest dinosaur that has been found is the supersaurus, but we still do not have a skeleton of the whole animal. Similar to the supersaurus is the brachiosaurus, which was a little bit smaller but still as tall as a five-story house. The front legs of these dinosaurs were longer than their hind legs. So the backs of these dinosaurs slanted down away from their heads.

They Ate a Lot—The supersaurus and the brachiosaurus were four-legged herbivores, with long necks and tails. Scientists believe that they ate like giraffes, with their necks up, munching the leaves on top of the taller plants and trees. To keep such big bodies alive, these large dinosaurs had to eat a huge amount of food. Their large bodies were supported by thick legs, just like elephants.

The brachiosaurus and the supersaurus were so tall that if they lived today, they would be able to look one another in the eye over the top of a modern train, and there would be room to spare.

In the Sea

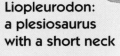

In the Sea—The large ancient reptiles that lived in the water were not dinosaurs. They were plesiosauruses. Instead of legs they had fins. Some had very long necks, like the elasmosaurus, which lived in deep water. Other plesiosauruses had shorter necks, like the liopleurodons. The ichthyosaurs were like dolphins. They could swim fast. They followed their prey—large octopuslike creatures with shells—and crushed them with their flat teeth. The females did not lay eggs, but gave birth to live offspring that were able to swim right away.

Other Giants—Other aquatic reptiles included turtles like the archelon, which was more than thirteen feet long. It had no teeth but had a very strong, pointed beak of horn. The tilosaurus was even longer, and had a large mouth with strong, knifelike teeth. It had a line of plates down its back like the crest of a dragon, a strong tail to push it through the water, and fins like the rudders of a submarine to give it direction.

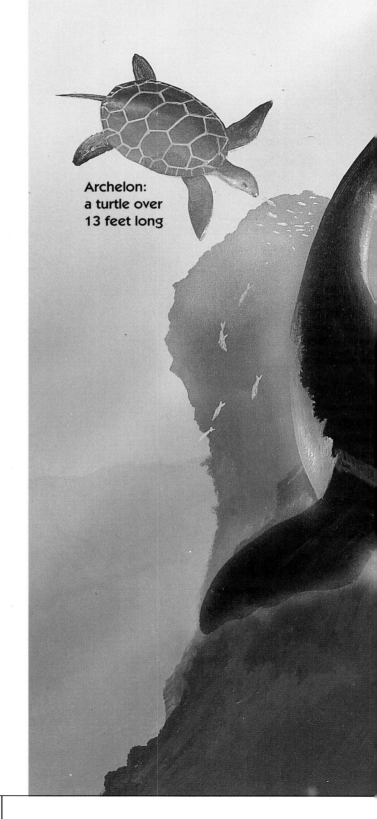

Archelon:
a turtle over
13 feet long

The ichthyosaurus was over 50 feet long.

Elasmosaurus: it had a small head and a long neck.

Shonisaurus: it had teeth only at the front of its long, pointy mouth.

Cryptoclidus: a plesiosaurus with a long neck

The Tilosaurus was more than 26 feet long.

Flying and Gliding

The long tail of the rhamphorhynchus made it more stable in flight, just like the tail of a kite.

Who Lived in the Sky?—For millions of years there were no birds. The only creatures that flew were insects. The first animals with an internal skeleton that could fly are called "pterosauruses." Attached to each side of its body was a wide piece of skin that formed a wing, like the wing of a bat. This wing was also sometimes attached to its tail. At the edge of the wing was a very long claw.

More Kites than Eagles— Pterosauruses were covered with very small hairs. These animals came in different sizes. Some were as small as swallows and some were as big as small airplanes. The muscles that pterosauruses used to fly were not as developed as those that birds use today.

The pterosaurus had a bony crest on its head that balanced its beak and toothless mouth.

Pterosauruses did not fly the way birds do. Instead of flapping their wings, pterosauruses jumped off high cliffs and glided on the wind, taking advantage of air currents. They glided over the sea to catch fish in their long beaklike mouths.

The Oldest Bird—The archaeopteryx had the body of a lizard, a long

The archaeopteryx is the oldest member of the bird family.

tail, and teeth. It lived 150 million years ago, and is considered to be the oldest bird. Its body was covered with feathers, and it was not related to the pterosauruses.

Armored and Armed

Instruments of Defense—Some dinosaurs were very heavily plated with something like horn or fingernails. Called "ankylosauruses," these animals had large, bony spikes and thick tails that ended in large knobs of bone. The plates on these armored animals were joined to one another, so the ankylosauruses could flex their backs. They could probably run very fast. Once they built up speed, it was difficult for them to stop, and they could accidentally knock over trees as well as destroy their enemies.

Like Armored Tanks—These heavily armed dinosaurs were all herbivores.

The ankylosaurus was more than thirty feet long and had an enormous hammer-shaped tail. It probably could have smashed a small armored tank.

Their plates defended them from predators. Most likely large carnivores tried to turn the ankylosauruses over on their backs, to attack their soft, unprotected stomachs.

A Dinosaur's Kiss

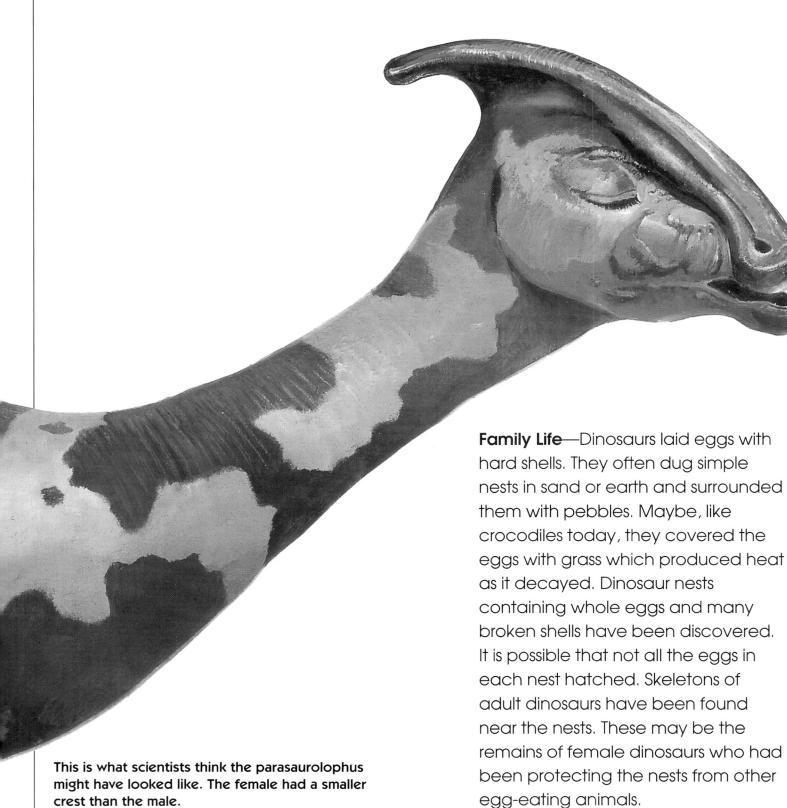

This is what scientists think the parasaurolophus might have looked like. The female had a smaller crest than the male.

Family Life—Dinosaurs laid eggs with hard shells. They often dug simple nests in sand or earth and surrounded them with pebbles. Maybe, like crocodiles today, they covered the eggs with grass which produced heat as it decayed. Dinosaur nests containing whole eggs and many broken shells have been discovered. It is possible that not all the eggs in each nest hatched. Skeletons of adult dinosaurs have been found near the nests. These may be the remains of female dinosaurs who had been protecting the nests from other egg-eating animals.

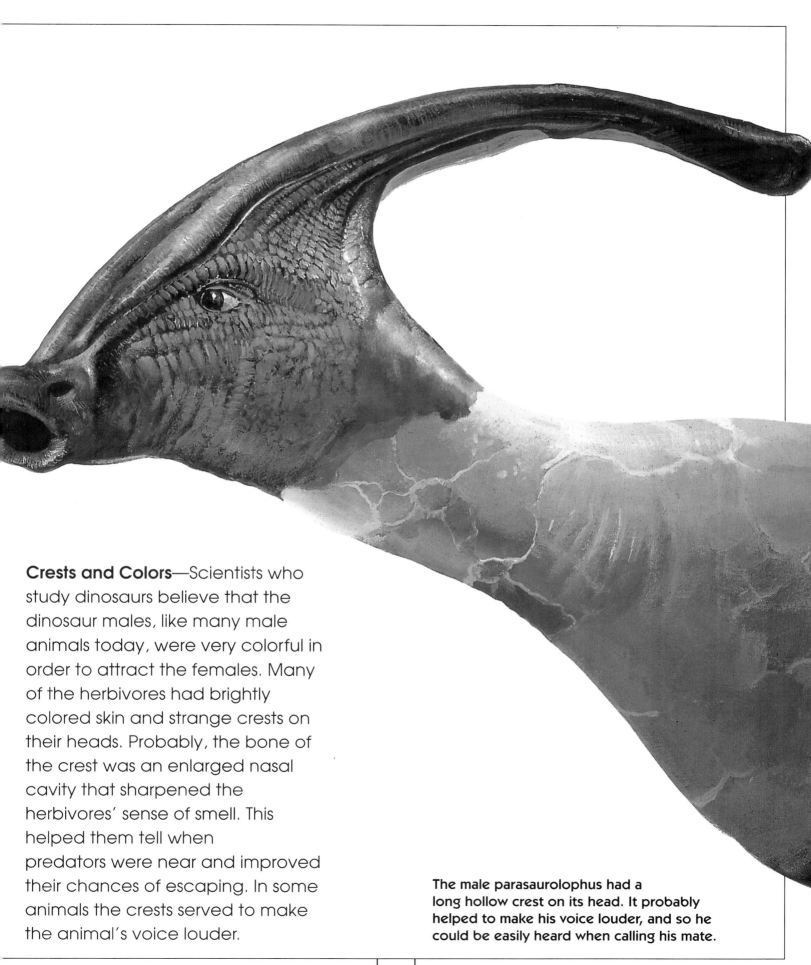

Crests and Colors—Scientists who study dinosaurs believe that the dinosaur males, like many male animals today, were very colorful in order to attract the females. Many of the herbivores had brightly colored skin and strange crests on their heads. Probably, the bone of the crest was an enlarged nasal cavity that sharpened the herbivores' sense of smell. This helped them tell when predators were near and improved their chances of escaping. In some animals the crests served to make the animal's voice louder.

The male parasaurolophus had a long hollow crest on its head. It probably helped to make his voice louder, and so he could be easily heard when calling his mate.

Eggs, Babies, and Mothers

The adult brachiosaurus weighed as much as ten elephants.

In the Egg—Even though many dinosaurs were huge, the largest dinosaur egg was probably only as big as the one pictured on the next page. Scientists believe that dinosaur babies grew fast and kept growing for the rest of their lives. They guess that the largest and heaviest adults were over 100 years old. Even though modern reptiles, like crocodiles and turtles, abandon their young, the ancient reptiles did not. Dinosaur mothers may have helped hatch the eggs and may have protected the babies when the family

moved from place to place. The babies came out of the egg fully able to walk.

Resistant but Fragile—The shell of a dinosaur egg had many tiny holes that let air in and harmful gases out (like a bird's egg). As the baby dinosaur developed, the shell became thinner and thinner as the substance it was made from was slowly absorbed by the growing baby.

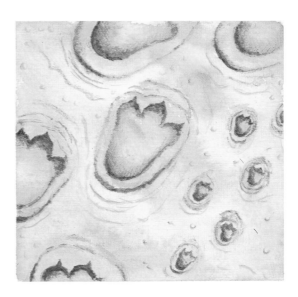

Footprints of adult dinosaurs have been found near those of the newly hatched babies. This shows that the mother dinosaurs did not abandon their young.

By the time the baby dinosaur was big enough to be born, the shell was thin enough for it to break—just like baby chicks today.

Dinosaur eggs had a hard shell that was slowly consumed from the inside as the baby dinosaur developed.

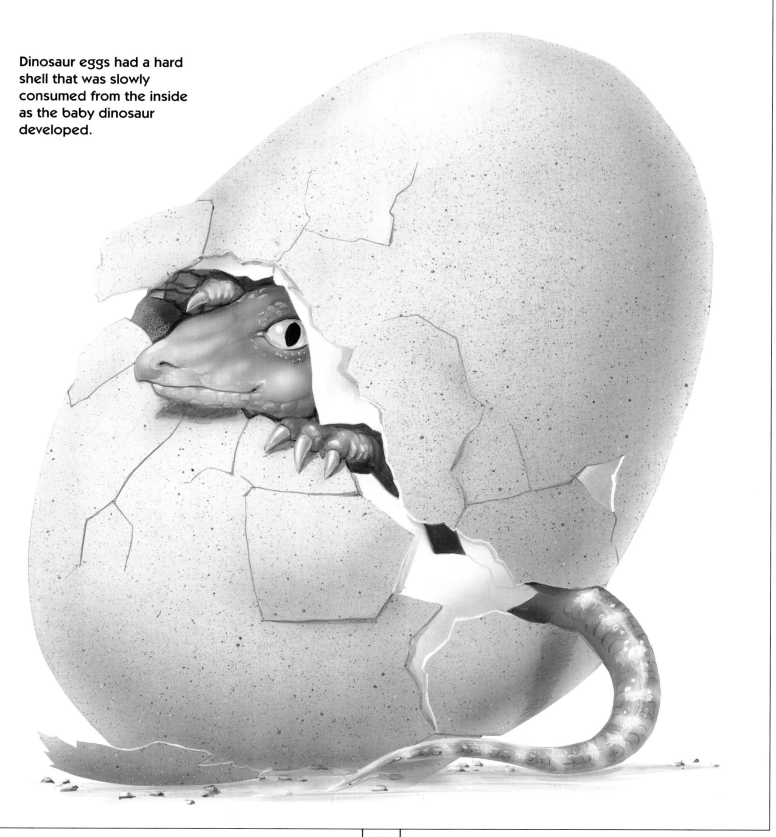

And Then They Disappeared

A Mystery—Dinosaurs became extinct 65 million years ago, long before humans appeared on the earth. The herbivore and carnivore dinosaurs, the marine reptiles, and the flying reptiles all disappeared, along with many kinds of sea and land plants. The survivors included insects, fish, mammals, other reptiles—including crocodiles and turtles—and also many different kinds of plants. What happened?

Many Explanations—There have been many theories about why the dinosaurs disappeared. One theory is that mammals ate all the dinosaur eggs, so there were no offspring. Another theory is that the dinosaurs got too large to be able to look for food. Today scientists think that a very drastic change happened in the earth's climate that caused many plants and animals to die. If the change did not cause the dinosaurs to die right away, it may have killed their food sources, which made the dinosaurs become extinct eventually.

Star Dust—The change in climate may have resulted from an asteroid (a small planetary body) that fell to earth. The asteroid crash may have caused a lot of dust to rain down, which blocked out the sun for a long time. That would have made the earth very cold—colder than the dinosaurs could have survived. Or maybe earthquakes and volcanic eruptions moved the continents and cooled the land and the oceans so much that the dinosaurs could not survive and they slowly disappeared.

Earth's History Continues

A Very Long Story—The history of the earth is very long. It began 4 1/2 billion years ago when the earth's surface was formed. Then 3 billion years ago the first living creatures (single-cell organisms) developed in the warm oceans that covered the planet. Very slowly, more complicated animals and plants developed.

did. Some, like the dinosaurs, became extinct and new animals took their places.

Mammals—Mammals developed about 200 million years ago from a group of very ancient reptiles that lived on the earth even before the dinosaurs. But mammals became numerous only after the dinosaurs had disappeared.

These are some of the animals that lived on the earth before humans. The first ones lived in the water and had very simple bodies. They were followed by reptiles, then dinosaurs and mammals, and finally primates.

The Planet's Evolution—At first the whole earth was covered with water. Then the oceans receded. The continents slowly moved away from each other—at the rate of about 1/2 inch per year. The climate changed from one extreme to the other: very cold periods in which the earth was covered with ice and snow were followed by very hot periods. So the animals and plants changed as their environments

Primates and Humans—Sixty million years ago, a new kind of mammal emerged: the primate. These animals had a very developed brain and eyes in the front of their heads. They were capable of climbing trees and were the ancestors of both humans and monkeys. Less than 2 million years ago (very recently in the long history of the earth), the first humans developed.

Our oldest human ancestor is Homo habillis, who lived in Africa about 2 million years ago.

COME SEE THE
WORLD OF
DINOSAURS

plateosaurus (flat lizard)—up to 30 feet long, walked more often on two feet than on four, lived 200 million years ago.

saltopus (foot that jumps)—just under 25 inches long, one of the smallest dinosaurs, biped, lived 190 million years ago.

compsognathus (nice mouth)—less than 25 inches long, as tall as a chicken, lived about 150 million years ago.

euparkeria (good animal of Parker)—less than 36 inches long, could walk on two legs or four, lived 220 million years ago.

ankylosaurus (lizard with joined armor)—over 33 feet long, herbivore, the biggest of the armored dinosaurs, lived 70 million years ago.

allosaurus (different lizard)—over 39 feet long, biped, carnivore, believed to be a terrible predator.

diplodocus ("double-beam," referring to the shape of the bones beneath its tail)—over 85 feet long, quadruped, herbivore.

Open and find something important. . .

They Still Exist

Dinosaurs have not completely disappeared from the earth. Their descendants live on, their "great-great-great-grandchildren"—the birds. If you compare the outline of a small dinosaur with that of a plucked chicken, you can see how similar they are. Birds also have scales like dinosaurs, but only on their feet. On the rest of their bodies, the scales have evolved into feathers.

. . . a dinosaur egg!

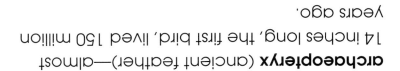

tyrannosaurus rex (lizard king)—almost 50 feet long, biped, carnivore, weighed 8 tons, lived 70 million years ago.

pteranodon (feather without teeth)—wingspan over 26 feet, a long crest behind its head, lived 75 million years ago.

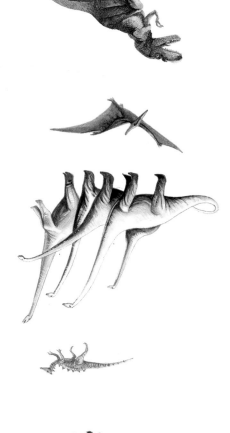

brachiosaurus (lizard with arms)—over 82 feet long, quadruped, herbivore, weighed 60 tons, lived 150 million years ago.

staurikosaurus (lizard with the "southern cross")—over 8 feet long, biped, predator, lived 250 million years ago.

cynodont (reptile like a mammal)—over 3 feet long, had whiskers on its face and hair all over its body, lived 220 million years ago.

stegosaurus (lizard with roof)—over 29 feet long, herbivore, had a row of large bony plates on each side of its backbone, lived 150 million years ago.

archaeopteryx (ancient feather)—almost 14 inches long, the first bird, lived 150 million years ago.

deinonychus (horrible claw)—over 13 feet long, biped with a rigid tail, carnivore and predator, lived 130 million years ago.

Family Portraits

The Tallest Crest—
The corythosaurus had
a very tall crest.

The Strangest—
The triceratops had horns on
its forehead and nose.

The Hardest Head—
The pachycephalosaurus
had a bone "helmet"
on its head.

The Slyest Thief—
The oviraptor stole the
eggs of other dinosaurs.

The Smallest—
The compsognathus weighed
as little as a baby.

The Noisiest—
The parasaurolophus
had a bone
"megaphone" on its head.

The Longest Teeth—
The tyrannosaurus rex
had 4-inch-long teeth.

The Fastest—
The velociraptor was the
fastest, on its two hind feet.

The Longest—
The diplodocus was over 90
feet long from head to tail.

Can They Come Back?

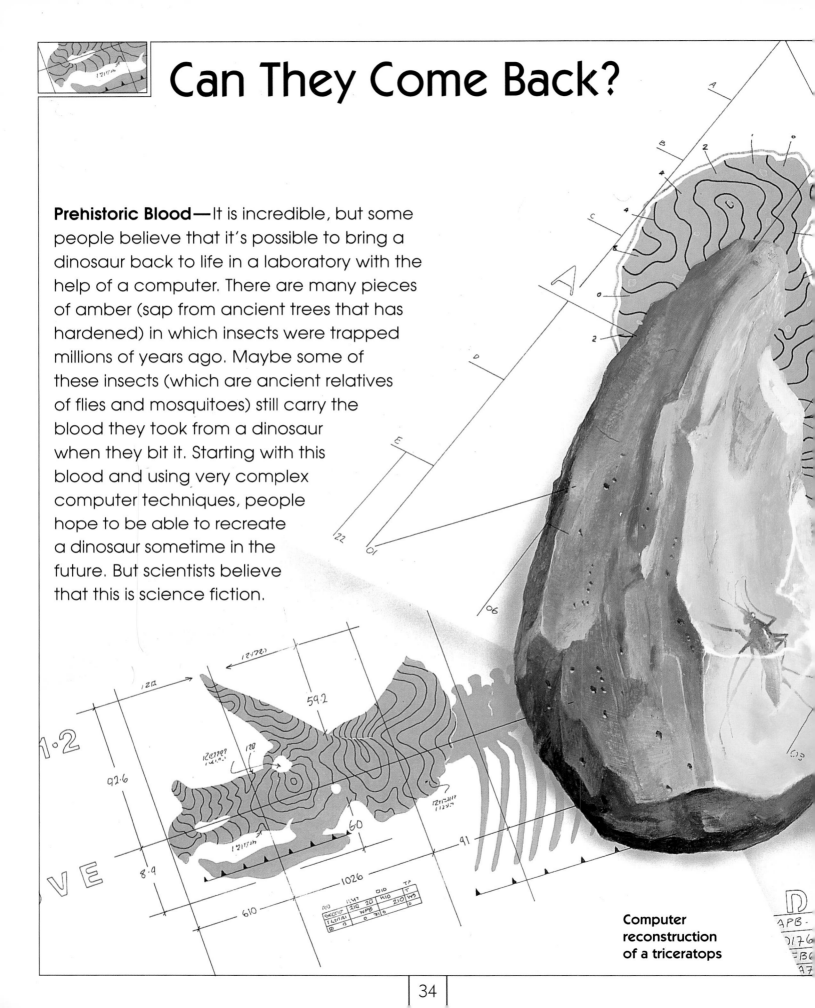

Prehistoric Blood—It is incredible, but some people believe that it's possible to bring a dinosaur back to life in a laboratory with the help of a computer. There are many pieces of amber (sap from ancient trees that has hardened) in which insects were trapped millions of years ago. Maybe some of these insects (which are ancient relatives of flies and mosquitoes) still carry the blood they took from a dinosaur when they bit it. Starting with this blood and using very complex computer techniques, people hope to be able to recreate a dinosaur sometime in the future. But scientists believe that this is science fiction.

Computer reconstruction of a triceratops

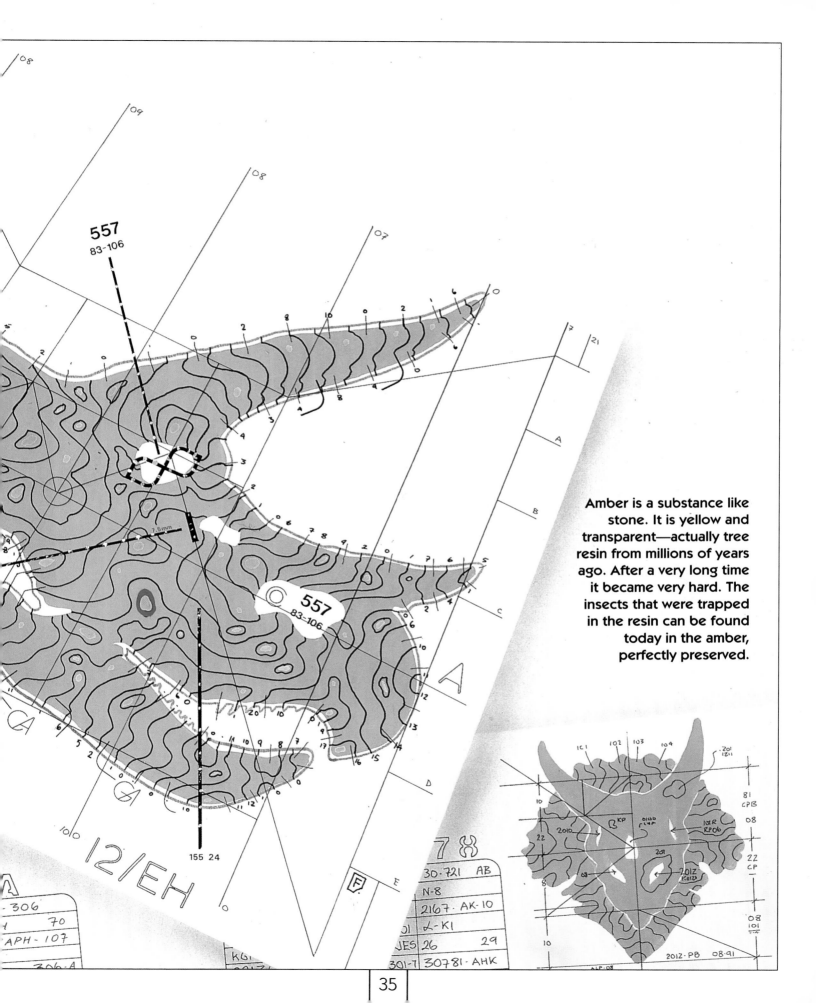

Amber is a substance like stone. It is yellow and transparent—actually tree resin from millions of years ago. After a very long time it became very hard. The insects that were trapped in the resin can be found today in the amber, perfectly preserved.

Dinosaur Hunting

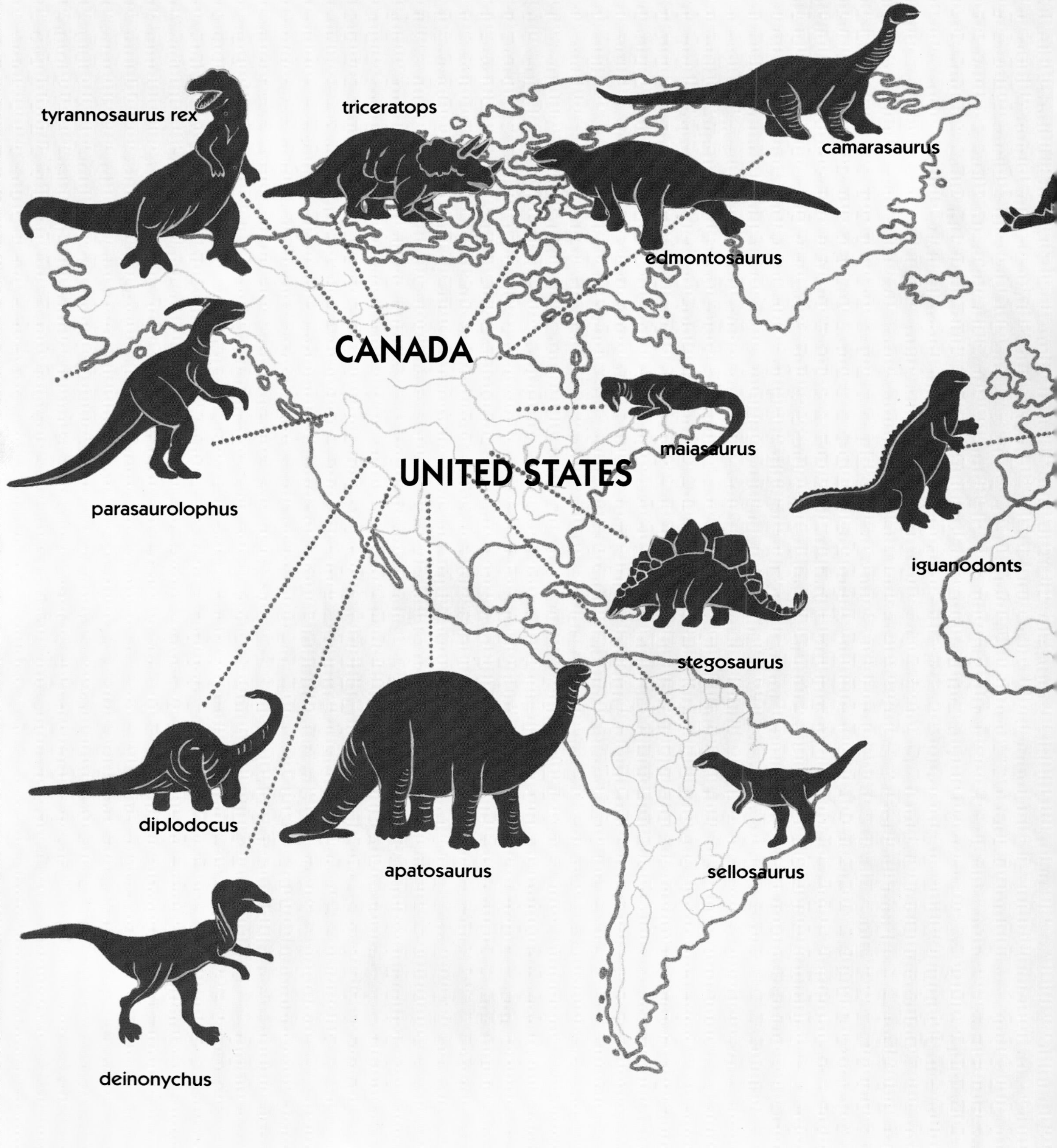

tyrannosaurus rex

triceratops

camarasaurus

edmontosaurus

CANADA

maiasaurus

UNITED STATES

parasaurolophus

iguanodonts

stegosaurus

diplodocus

apatosaurus

sellosaurus

deinonychus

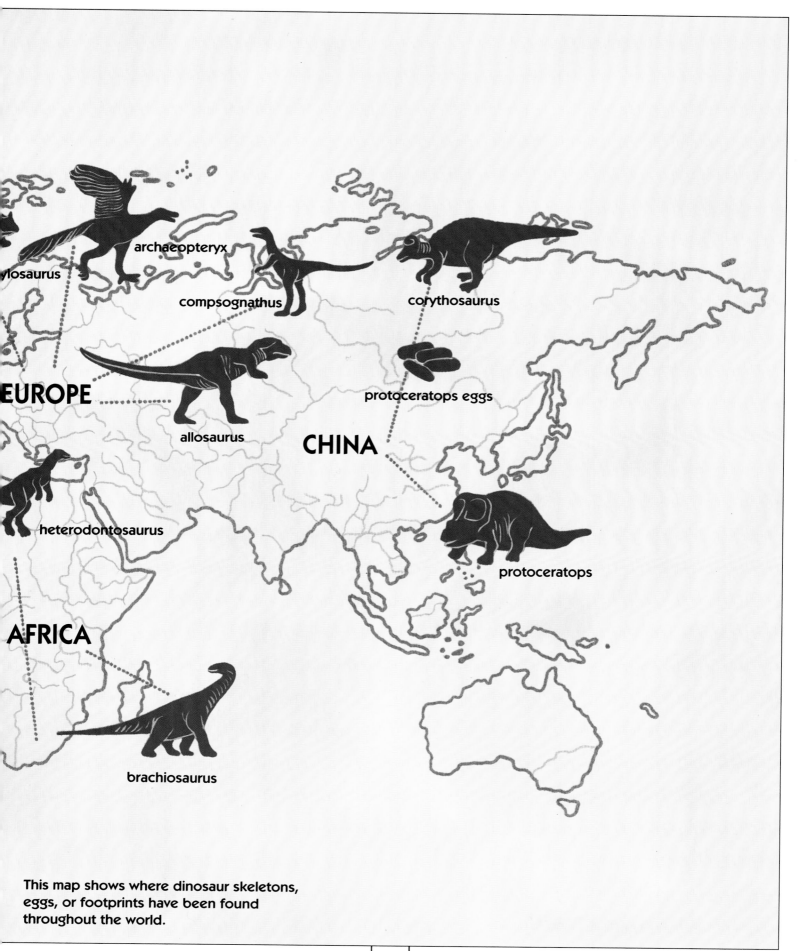

archaeopteryx

...ylosaurus

compsognathus

corythosaurus

EUROPE

allosaurus

protoceratops eggs

CHINA

heterodontosaurus

protoceratops

AFRICA

brachiosaurus

This map shows where dinosaur skeletons,
eggs, or footprints have been found
throughout the world.

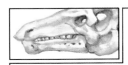

In the Museum

Like a Puzzle— Today you can see dinosaurs at a natural history museum. After a dinosaur skeleton has been dug up, it is taken to a laboratory where it is carefully cleaned. Then the work of a paleontologist begins. Paleontologists are people who study the remains of ancient plants and animals. They compare any new specimens they find with the skeletons of dinosaurs that have already been examined and classified. Once the paleontologists have classified the specimen, they lay out all its bones like a giant puzzle. The bones are attached to a metal frame that holds them in place. If some of the bones are missing, replicas of the missing bones are made out of plastic or plaster. Then all the bones are coated with a chemical to protect them from the atmosphere. Then the skeleton is ready to display in the museum.

As Good as Real— Some dinosaurs that are in museums have had their muscles, skin, and scales reconstructed over their bones. In that way they look as if they could walk right off the stand.

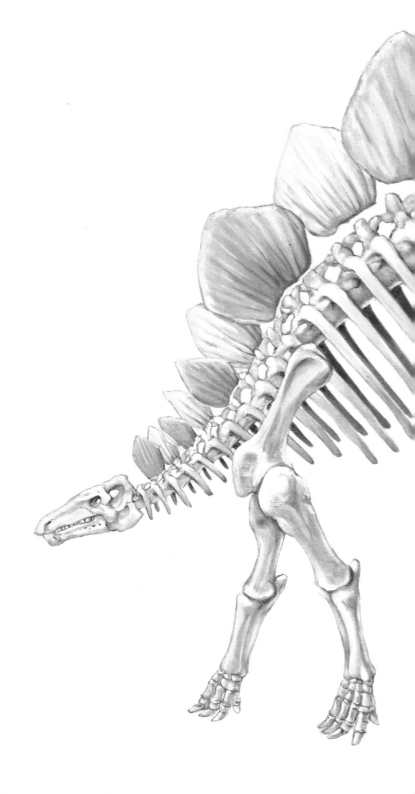

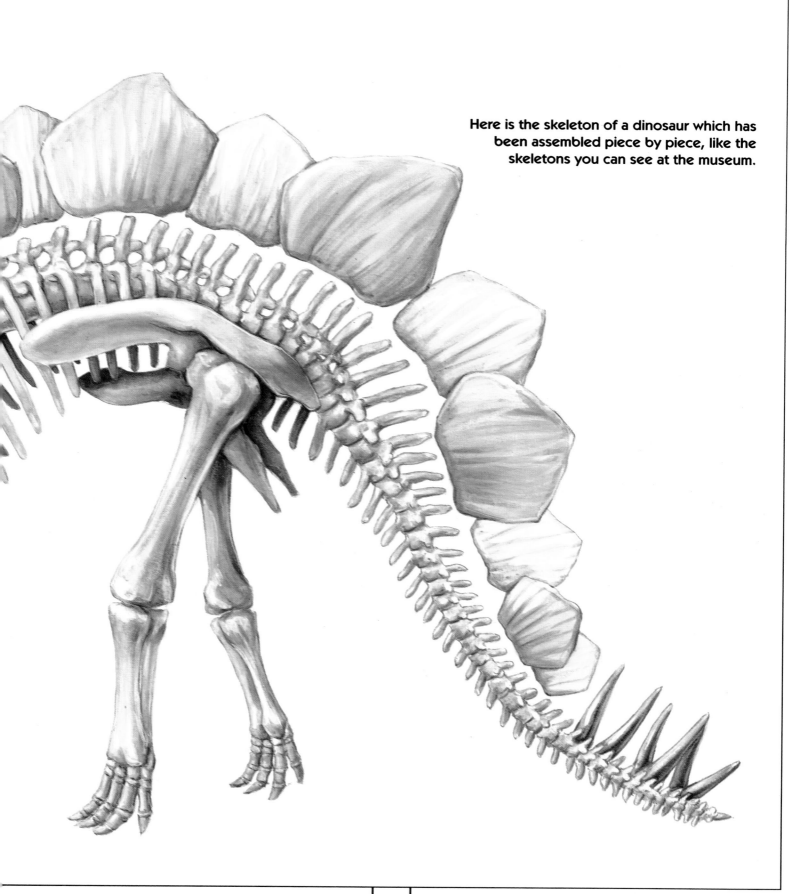

Here is the skeleton of a dinosaur which has been assembled piece by piece, like the skeletons you can see at the museum.

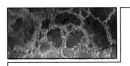

I Dreamed About a Monster

Giants and Dragons—Even in ancient times people found remains of dinosaurs that had lived a long time before them. They must have tried to imagine what kinds of animals these dinosaurs were. How big was the animal whose teeth or skull or bones they found? From their imaginings, stories evolved about monstrous creatures that lived in lost valleys, in lakes, in caves, or in the seas. These monsters frightened lost travelers, sailors, and even entire populations.

The Loch Ness Monster—Today people still talk of monsters they claim to have seen or photographed. The most famous of modern-day monsters is Nessie, the monster who is supposed to live in the deep waters of Loch Ness in Scotland. People who believe that Nessie exists think it might be a prehistoric reptile with fins like the plesiosaurus. Nobody has ever managed to get a photograph of Nessie, and scientists think that the Loch Ness Monster is a figment of people's imaginations.

What Color Were They?

Not Just Fantasy— Scientists think that dinosaurs may have had brightly colored skin. They base this idea on the fact that many modern reptiles do. Coral snakes have bright red, black, and yellow stripes. Gila monsters have pink and black markings. Capri lizards are completely blue. Chameleons can change color in order to blend in with their environment.

So it is possible that dinosaur skin was also multicolored or spotted. Dinosaurs (especially the herbivores and small dinosaurs) needed to hide from their enemies. Scientists have considered some colors that dinosaurs might have been. They kept in mind the colors of the plants around the dinosaurs that they might have eaten, and the color of the sand where they laid their eggs. Imagine a blue, green, or red stegosaurus!

Blue stegosaurus—it could have blended in with seawater.

Green stegosaurus—this dinosaur would have been camouflaged in the forest.

Red stegosaurus—this color might have frightened off its enemies.

An ABC of Dinosaurs

A as in Apatosaurus— Large quadruped dinosaur. It was mostly vegetarian. It used to be called "brontosaurus."

B as in Birds—Animals with upper limbs for flying. They evolved from the small biped carnivores. The first bird appeared about 150 million years ago.

C as in Ceratopsids— Group of herbivore dinosaurs with collars and horns. The most famous is the triceratops.

D as in Dinosaur—The dinosaurs, or "terrible lizards," appeared on earth about 230 million years ago and became extinct about 65 million years ago.

E as in Erect—The way some biped dinosaurs walked. Standing upright.

F as in Frill—The name for the bony face and neck covering on some horned dinosaurs, such as the protoceratops.

G as in Gallimimus—A very agile predatory biped dinosaur. Much like an ostrich in gait.

H as in Homo sapiens— The scientific name for modern people. It means "wise man."

I as in Ichthyosaur—Extinct marine reptiles. They lived at the same time as the dinosaurs. Perfectly

adapted to deep water, they did not lay eggs. They gave birth to live young, just like mammals.

J as in Jurassic—One of three periods when dinosaurs lived. The others are Triassic and Cretaceous.

K as in Kuehneosaurus—A gliding dinosaur that lived during the Triassic period.

L as in Limbs—The upper limbs of an animal correspond to human arms and the hind limbs to human legs.

M as in Mass extinction— The period when a whole species becomes extinct. This happened to the dinosaurs.

N as in Nest—Many baby dinosaurs were hatched from eggs deposited in nests.

O as in Ornitholestes—A carnivore, it was one of the smallest dinosaurs. It was as tall as a ten-year-old child.

P as in Pentaceratops—Penta means "five" but the pentaceratops did not have five real horns. Two of them were just long bones on its face.

Q as in Quadrupeds—are animals that walk on four legs. Bipeds walk on two legs.

R as in Rhynchosaur—A squat dinosaur with a hooked beak.

S as in Sauropod—A large quadruped dinosaur with a long neck, and a small head. A herbivore, it had thick legs and feet, like an elephant.

T as in Tyrannosaurus—The biggest of the carnivorous dinosaurs. It was a biped that might have been a hunter, but scientists believe it was probably a scavenger.

U as in Ultrasaurus—It is believed that this dinosaur might have been more than 98 feet long.

V as in Velociraptor—A carnivorous dinosaur that could run very fast.

W as in Wing—The first flying dinosaurs were gliders. They did not flap their wings as birds do today.

X as in Xiaosaurus—One of the smallest biped dinosaurs.

Y as in Young—At one time scientists thought that dinosaurs did not look after their young. But we now know that some of them did.

Z as in Zygorhiza—An early whale whose head was separated from its body by a distinct neck.

Glossary

adapt—adjust to a new environment.

evolution—how a species changes to survive over time.

amphibian—an animal that lives the first part of its life in the water and the second part on land.

biology—the study of living things.

biped—an animal that walks on two legs.

camouflage—to blend in with background colors or shapes so you cannot be seen.

carnivore—a meat eater.

carnosaur—a meat-eating dinosaur.

environment—all the conditions (plants, animals, and climate) that affect a living thing.

extinct—when no living individuals of a species remain.

fossil—the remains of a prehistoric plant or animal, or its imprint in rock.

geology—the study of the formation of the earth.

gills—membranes or slits through which fish breathe the oxygen that is in water.

herbivore—a plant eater.

invertebrate—an animal with no backbone (insects, spiders, and worms).

mammal—a warm-blooded animal that gives birth to live young.

offspring—babies.

omnivore—an animal that eats both plants and animals.

organism—any kind of plant or animal life.

paleontologist—someone who studies fossils of plants and animals that lived in prehistoric times.

petrified—turned to stone.

physiology—the study of how animals and plants function.

predator—an animal that lives by eating the animals it kills.

prehistoric—before recorded human history.

primates—a group of animals that includes humans, apes, and monkeys.

quadruped—an animal that walks on four legs.

reptile—a cold-blooded animal that crawls.

resin—sap from plants or trees.

scavenger—an animal that lives by eating already dead animals.

skeleton—the bony framework of a vertebrate animal.

species—a group of animals or plants that are very similar to each other. They produce offspring that can reproduce as well. In this way, the species will last a long time—longer than the lifespan of an individual.

vertebrate—an animal with a backbone (mammals, birds, reptiles, amphibians, and fish).